W9-ATB-355

Let's Talk About When You Think Nobody Likes You

Melanie Ann Apel

The Rosen Publishing Group's
PowerKids Press™
New York

For Dad, who has always liked me for the person I am

Published in 2002 by The Rosen Publishing Group, Inc.
29 East 21st Street, New York, NY 10010

First Edition

Book Design: Emily Muschinske
Project Editors: Jason Moring, Jennifer Landau

Photographs by Kate Preftakes except p. 11 © Skjold.

Apel, Melanie Ann.
    Let's talk about when you think nobody likes you / Melanie Ann Apel. —1st ed.
        p. cm. —(The let's talk about library)
Includes index.
    ISBN 0-8239-5862-0 (library binding)
    1. Self-esteem in children—Juvenile literature. 2. Self-perception in children—Juvenile literature.
[1. Self-esteem. 2. Self-perception.]
    [DNLM: 1. Self Concept—Child—Juvenile Literature. 2. Negativism—Child—Juvenile Literature.
WS 105.5.S3 A641L 2002] I. Title II. Series.
    BF723.S3 A64 2002
    155.4'18—dc21
                                                                    00–012076

Manufactured in the United States of America

Contents

When You Have a Bad Day

Once in a while you may have a bad day. Perhaps you want to play with someone and no one is there. Maybe your mom is very busy and she doesn't have time to spend with you. If you're having a bad day, you may not feel very good about yourself. You may think that others don't like you. When Gavin is having a bad day, he doesn't share his toys with his sister, Helen. This makes Helen think that Gavin doesn't like her. Sometimes this makes Helen sad. Helen tries to understand that Gavin is just having a bad day.

◀ *Sometimes when we are alone, we may start to think that something is wrong with us. This can make us feel lonely.*

Claire's Hurt Feelings

Claire is feeling sad today. Her brothers, Jeff and Scott, won't let her play ball with them. This makes Claire lonely. Her friend Dana went to play at Ella's house. Claire wasn't invited to join them. Claire feels jealous and hurt. Claire's sister Mia went to the zoo with their Aunt Jane. Now Claire is angry. She doesn't think it's fair that Mia gets a special day with Aunt Jane. Claire hugs her dog, Buttons. Buttons wags his tail. "How come nobody likes me?" Claire asks him. It's not a good feeling when you think nobody likes you.

Claire is very angry because she is jealous of her sister. When we are angry at ▶ *others, we might push them away.*

The First Day of School

Andy will be going to a new school in a new neighborhood. He is afraid that kids in his new school won't like him. He likes his old school. He has a lot of friends there. Andy tells his parents he does not want to go to the new school. His parents tell him not to worry. They point out that he made many friends at his old school, and he will be able to make many new friends at the new school. His sister Belle tells him that she is not afraid of going to a new school. Belle is excited about all of the new friends she is going to make. Belle's **attitude** is different from Andy's.

It is normal to feel nervous about meeting new ◄ *people. Andy's mother tries to comfort him before his first day at a new school.*

9

Being Kind to Others

Erika has been **moping** around the house. "Nobody likes me," Erika tells her mom. Her mom tells her that this is not true at all. "I like you," her mom tells her. "Dad and Natalie like you." She lists Erika's favorite playmates. Erika just feels as though nobody likes her. The truth is that she has many friends and a lot of people like her. People like Erika because she is kind to others. Everyone likes people who are kind. Being kind means helping other people, being nice, and sharing. Sometimes it is good to be reminded of all the people who like you.

If you treat people kindly, they will be happier around you. ▶

Bad Behavior

Has anyone ever told you that he or she doesn't like you? Those are hard words to hear. Were you misbehaving? Sometimes people do things that they know are wrong. It can be hard to get along with someone who doesn't act nicely. It makes it hard for people to like you if you throw tantrums, act meanly, or are selfish or uncooperative. People won't stop liking you if you are moody or misbehave once in a while. Everyone has bad days and makes mistakes. Make sure you try to act nicely most of the time, though. People like others who are polite and kind.

◀ *Everyone says or does things they wish they could take back. If we treat others with kindness, we will receive kindness in return.*

Self-Esteem

Self-esteem is how you think of yourself. Colleen feels good when she takes care of her little sister, Molly. Colleen also feels proud when she does well on a math test. Colleen has high self-esteem because she has healthy feelings about what she does and how she acts. She feels **confident** about what she can do. Ben practices his violin every day, but he never thinks his music sounds good enough. When Ben does well on a math test, he only thinks about how he could have done better. Ben has low self-esteem. He does not have very good feelings about himself.

Ben has a hard time feeling good about himself. No matter how well he does, he always thinks he should do better. ▶

Understanding Your Feelings

If you think nobody likes you, there must be a good reason for this feeling. Maybe no one talks to you at lunch. Maybe you're left out of games. Think about why these things are happening. Did you hurt someone's feelings? Did you do something mean? You may have done something without even knowing it. You can **resolve** this kind of **misunderstanding**. Talk to the other kids. Make the first move by being friendly. You will feel better when you have made new friends or cleared up disagreements with old friends.

◄ *Feeling left out can be very hard. Still, we should try to talk to others and understand their feelings as well as our own.*

Being Shy

Howard watches other kids playing in the park after school. He wants to join them, but he's too shy to ask. Howard doesn't like to talk to kids that he doesn't know. He is afraid they'll say they don't want him to play. He is also afraid that they won't like him. Howard stands near the kids, hoping they will ask him to join them. One day, Jenny notices Howard and asks him to play with them. "I thought you didn't like me because you never asked me before," Howard says. Jenny tells Howard that the kids thought Howard didn't like them because he never joined them!

Other people can mistake shyness for rudeness. It is important to be open to making new friends. ▶

Having Friends

Some kids have many friends. Some kids have just a few close friends. Either way is fine. The number of friends you have is not important. It is important that you are kind to others and to yourself. If you like who you are, you will feel good about yourself. If you feel good about yourself, other people will feel good about you, too. If others feel good about you, it will be easy to make friends. If you are friendly and fun, and if you share toys and **cooperate**, it is likely that you will have many friends.

◀ *Friendship is one of the things that makes life special. Before we can make friends, though, we have to like ourselves.*

Liking Yourself

If you like yourself, chances are that others will like you, too. Sometimes you may think that nobody likes you. It's normal to feel like this once in a while. If you feel like this a lot, you may need to change your attitude. You may need to be more accepting of other people. You may need to make a bigger effort to understand other people's feelings. If you are really worried that somebody doesn't like you, ask that person. Remember that many people do like you, care about you, and love you a lot!

Glossary

attitude (A-tuh-tood) How you feel toward things.

confident (KON-fih-dent) Believing in yourself and your abilities.

cooperate (koh-AH-puh-rayt) To work well with others.

misunderstanding (mih-sun-der-STAN-ding) Failure to understand.

moping (MOH-ping) Feeling unhappy without trying to feel better.

resolve (rih-ZAHLV) To find an answer or work things out.

self-esteem (self-eh-STEEM) How you feel about yourself.

Index